Book One

CLASSICS *for* PIANO DUET

7 Duet Arrangements of Student Favorites for Late Elementary to Early Intermediate Pianists

George Peter TINGLEY

Classics for Piano Duet, Book 1, contains seven familiar piano classics arranged as fun student duets. The original solo versions may lie beyond the reach of early-grade pianists, but they are immediately accessible in these rich-sounding, four-hand arrangements arranged for late-elementary to early-intermediate pianists. When possible, the original key of the piece has been maintained; however, some pieces have been transposed to facilitate the learning process. All retain the integrity of the original solo. In these duets, students not only gain valuable ensemble experience, but they also explore music that they eventually may play as solos.

This collection contains sparkling arrangements of such favorites as Johann Sebastian Bach's *Menuet in G Major* (BWV Anh. 114) and Scott Joplin's *Maple Leaf Rag.* Effective recital programming could include the original solo version followed by the duet from this book. Students will enjoy getting acquainted with these great works through these musical arrangements!

George Peter Tingley

Alfred

Menuet in G Major

from the Notebook for Anna Magdalena

SECONDO

Johann Sebastian Bach (1685–1750)

Arr. by George Peter Tingley

Allegro moderato

Play both hands one octave lower than written throughout

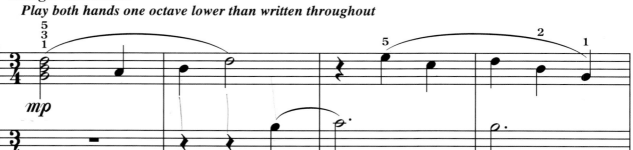

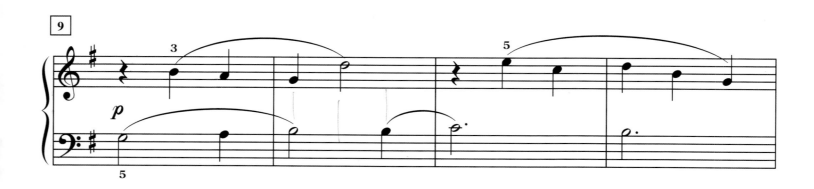

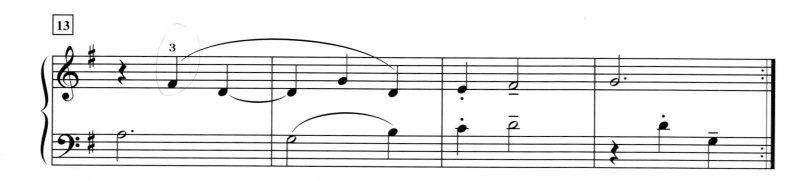

Menuet in G Major

from the Notebook for Anna Magdalena

PRIMO

Johann Sebastian Bach (1685–1750)
Arr. by George Peter Tingley

Allegro moderato
Play both hands one octave higher than written throughout

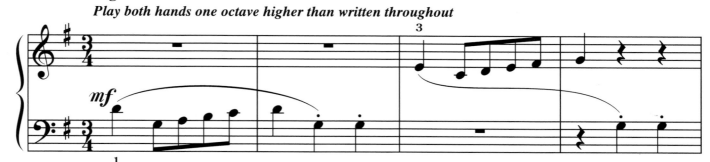

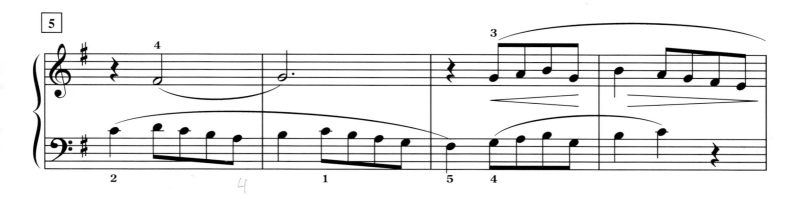

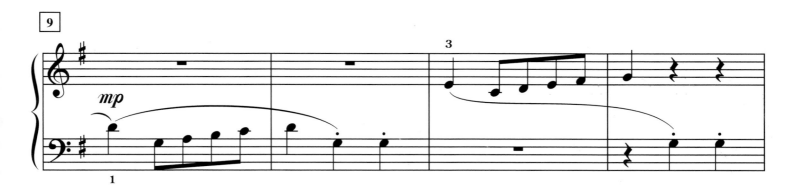

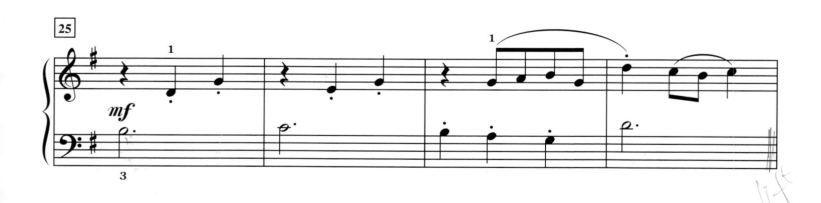

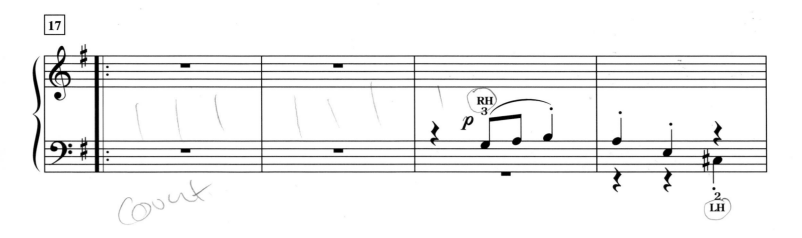

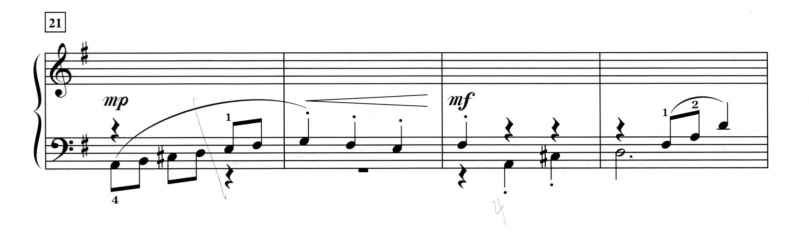

German Dance

SECONDO

Franz Joseph Haydn (1732–1809)
Arr. by George Peter Tingley

Allegretto
Play both hands one octave lower than written throughout

German Dance

PRIMO

Franz Joseph Haydn (1732–1809)
Arr. by George Peter Tingley

Allegretto

Play both hands one octave higher than written throughout

Ecossaise
WoO 23

SECONDO

Ludwig van Beethoven (1770–1827)
Arr. by George Peter Tingley

Allegro
Play both hands one octave lower than written throughout

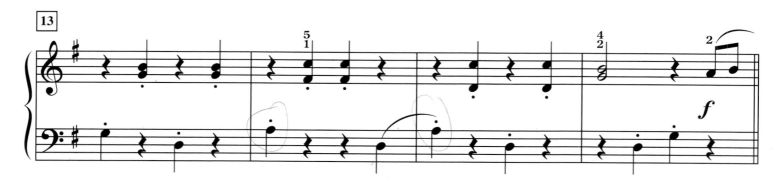

Ecossaise
WoO 23

PRIMO

Ludwig van Beethoven (1770–1827)
Arr. by George Peter Tingley

Allegro
Play both hands one octave higher than written throughout

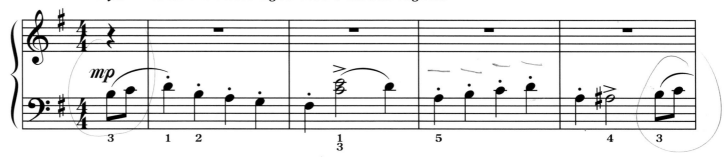
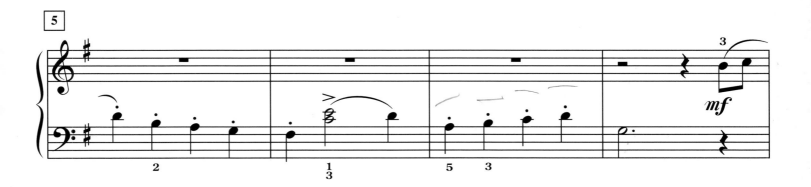
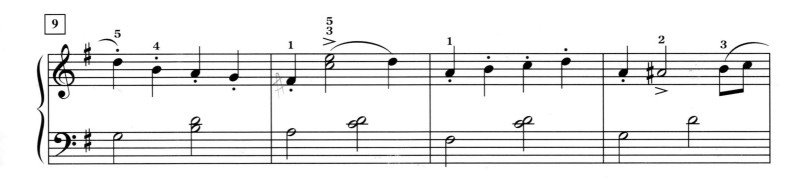
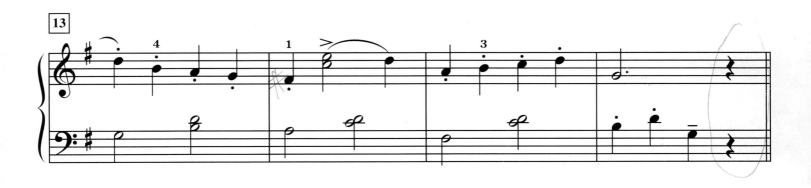

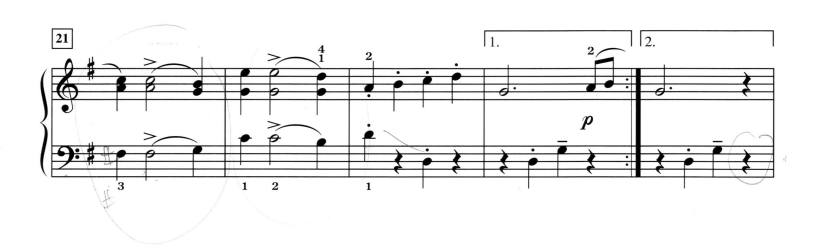

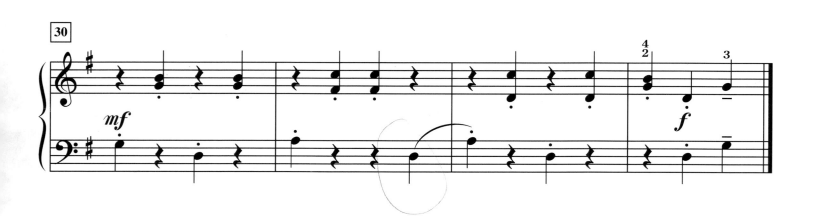

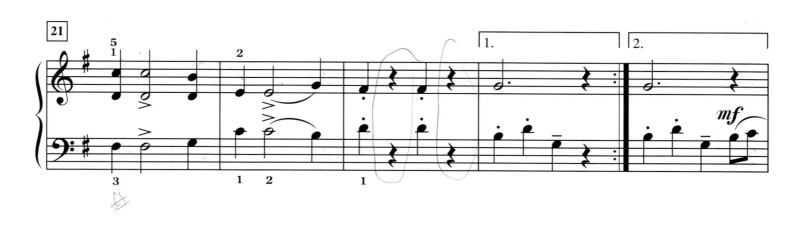

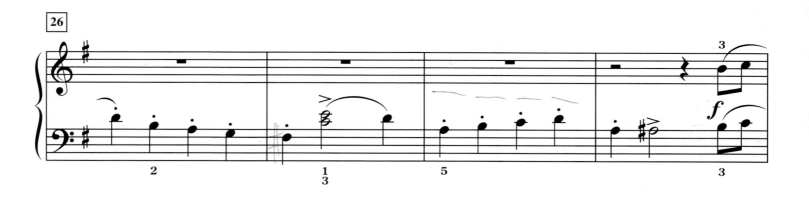

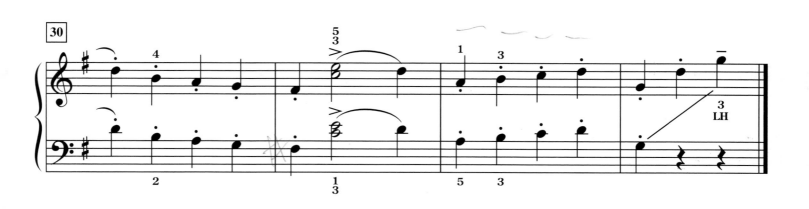

Bagatelle

Op. 125, No. 10

SECONDO

Anton Diabelli (1781–1858)
Arr. by George Peter Tingley

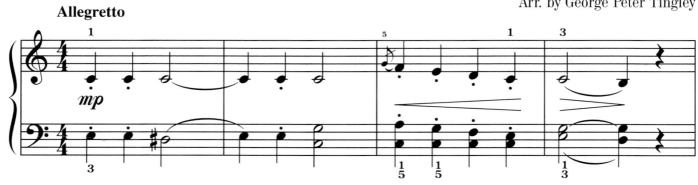

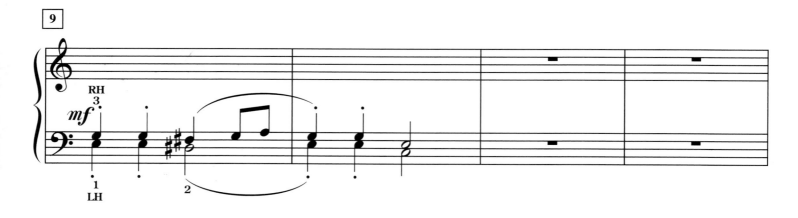

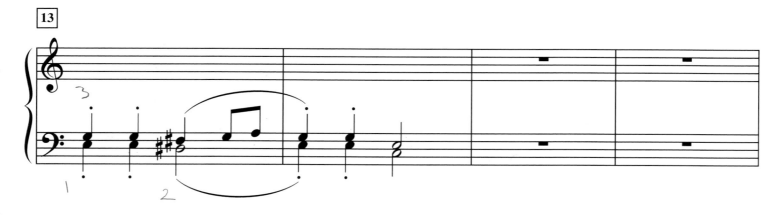

Bagatelle

Op. 125, No. 10

PRIMO

Anton Diabelli (1781–1858)

Arr. by George Peter Tingley

Allegretto

Play both hands one octave higher than written throughout

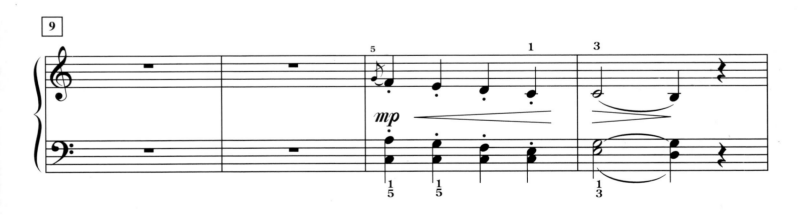

17 *Play both hands one octave lower than written to the end*

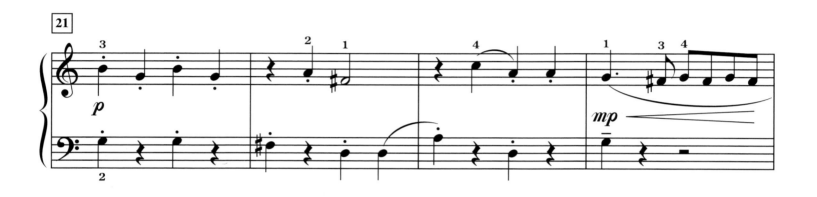

21

25

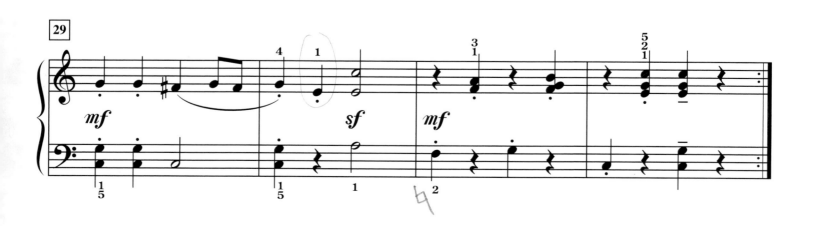

29

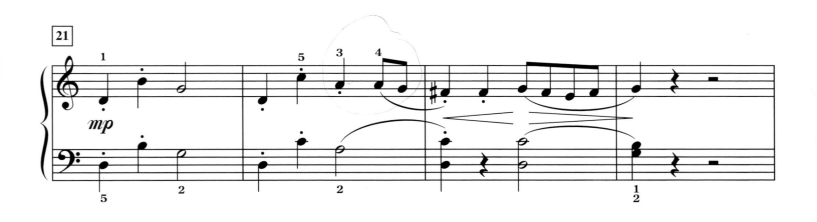

Sonatina in C Major
Op. 36, No. 1
First Movement

SECONDO

Muzio Clementi (1753–1832)
Arr. by George Peter Tingley

Allegro

Play both hands one octave lower than written throughout

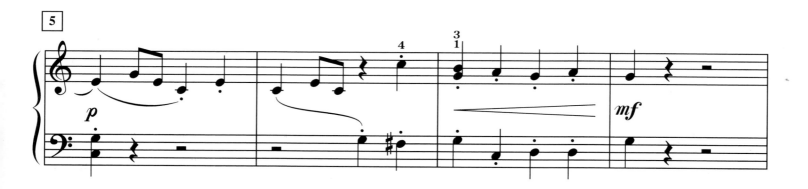

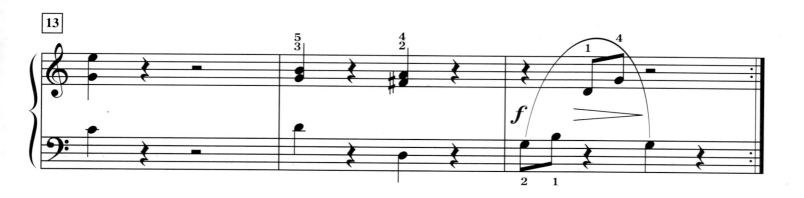

Sonatina in C Major

Op. 36, No. 1
First Movement

PRIMO

Muzio Clementi (1753–1832)
Arr. by George Peter Tingley

Allegro
Play both hands one octave higher than written throughout

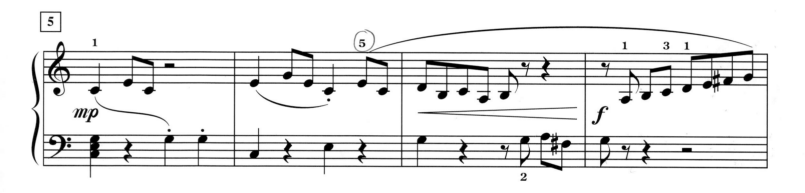

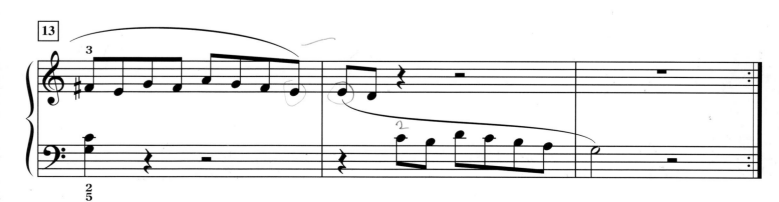

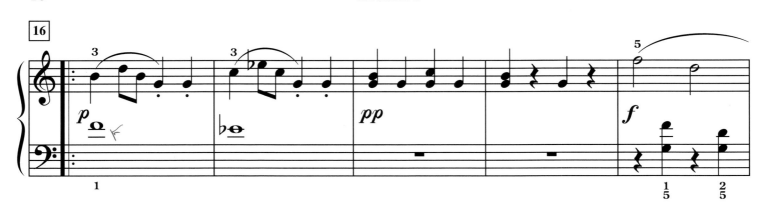

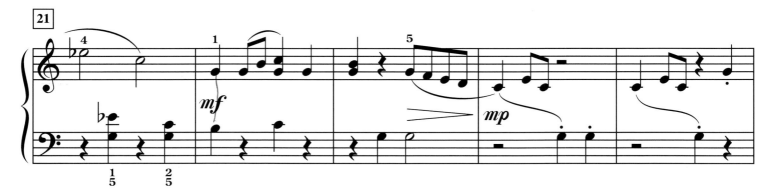

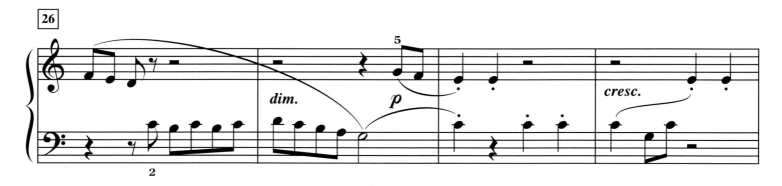

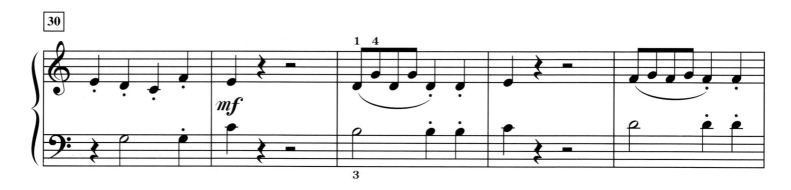

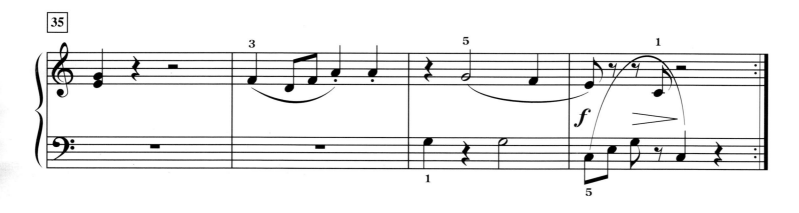

Melody in F
Op. 3, No. 1

SECONDO

Anton Rubinstein (1829–1894)
Arr. by George Peter Tingley

Moderato
Play both hands one octave lower than written throughout

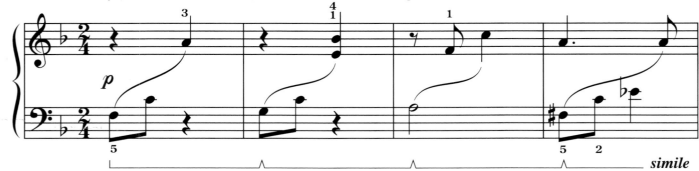

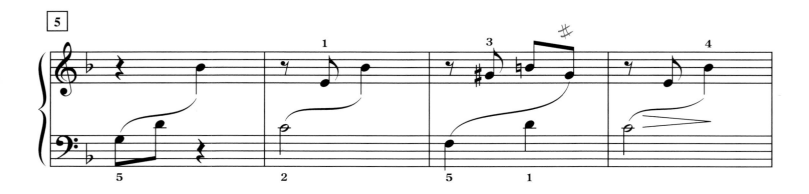

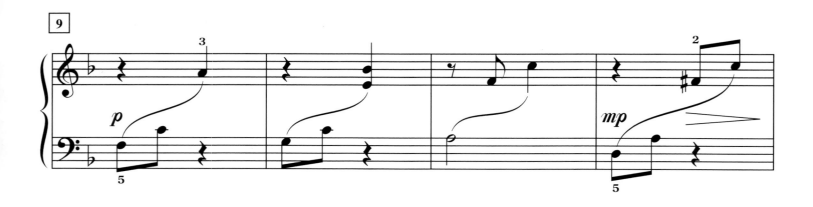

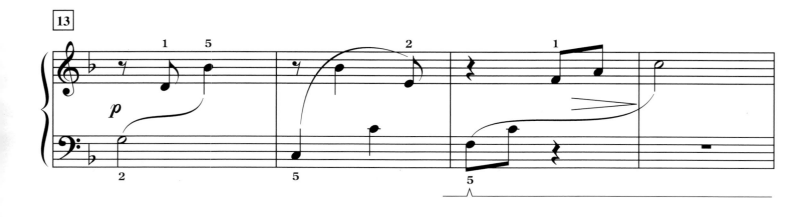

Melody in F

Op. 3, No. 1

PRIMO

Anton Rubinstein (1829–1894)
Arr. by George Peter Tingley

Moderato
Play both hands one octave higher than written throughout

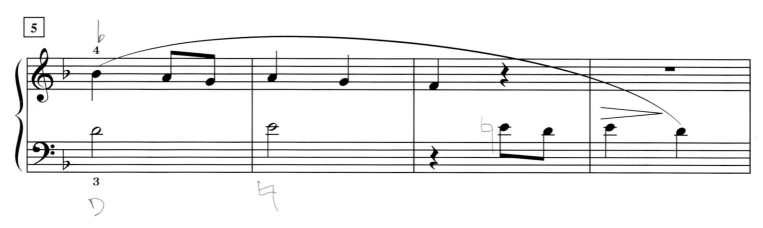

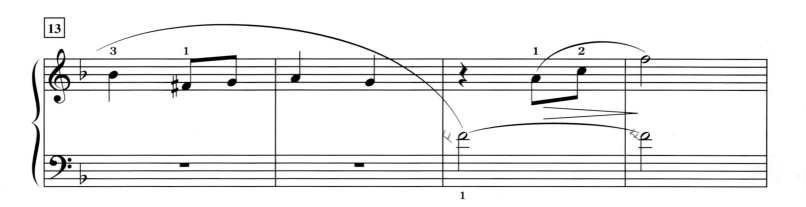

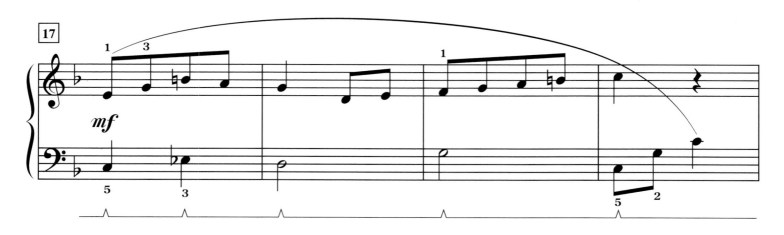

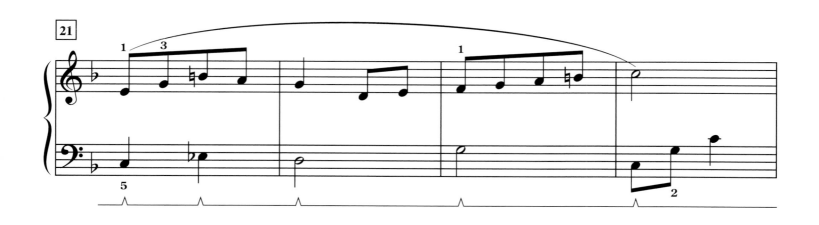

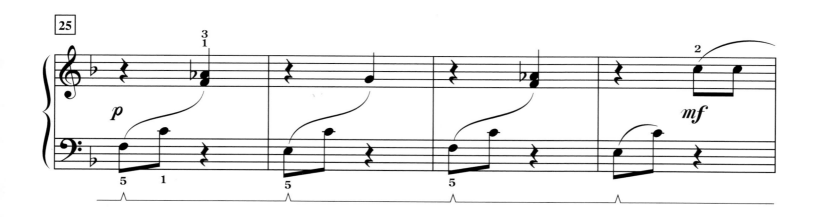

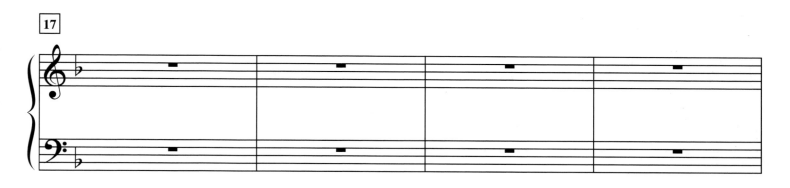

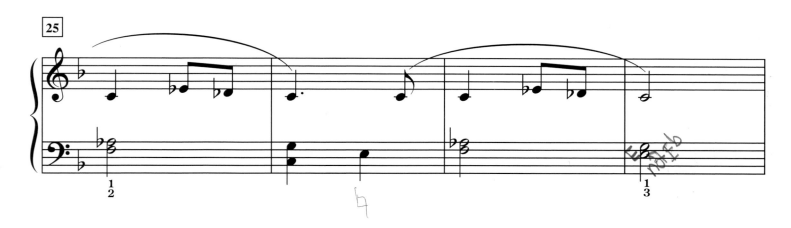

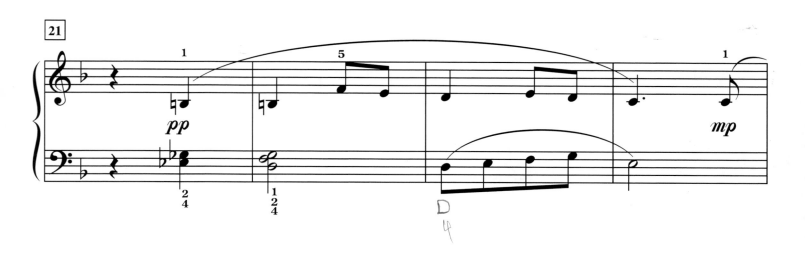

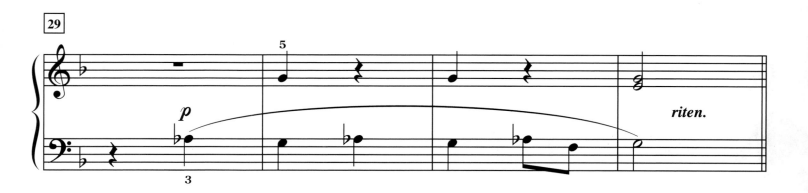

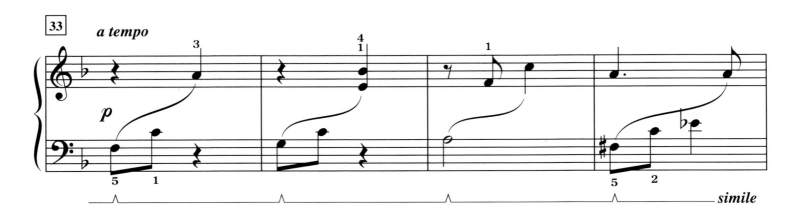

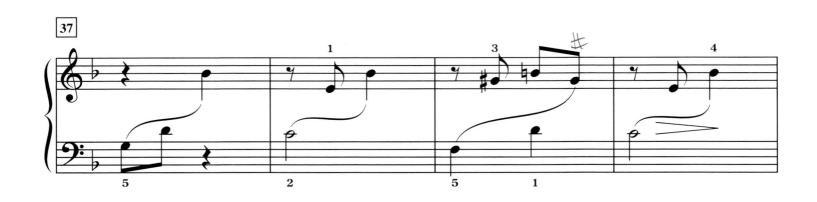

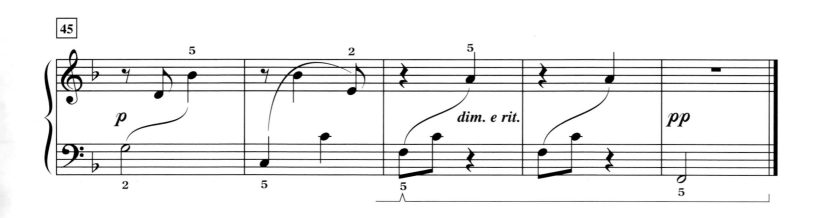

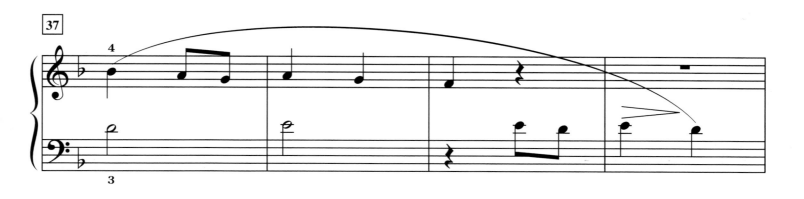

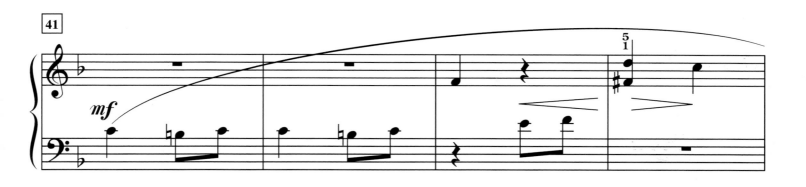

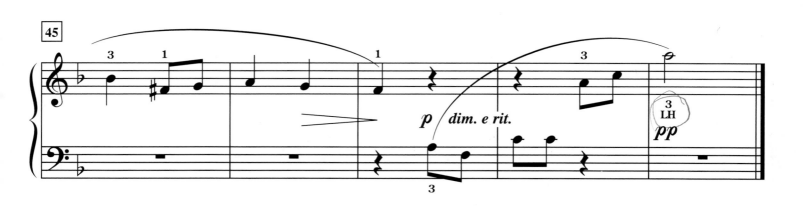

Maple Leaf Rag

SECONDO

Scott Joplin (1868–1917)
Arr. by George Peter Tingley

Tempo di marcia
Play both hands one octave lower than written throughout

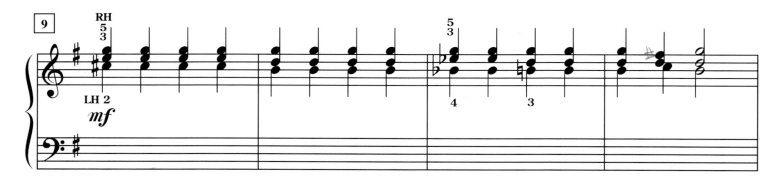

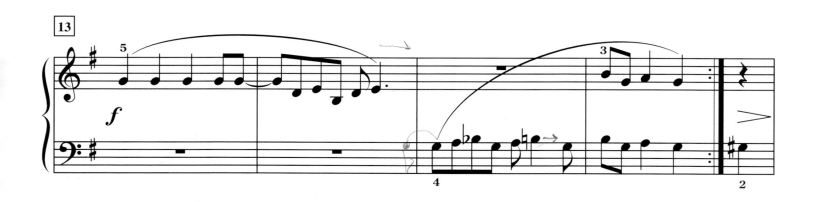

Maple Leaf Rag

PRIMO

Scott Joplin (1868–1917)
Arr. by George Peter Tingley

Tempo di marcia
Play both hands one octave higher than written throughout

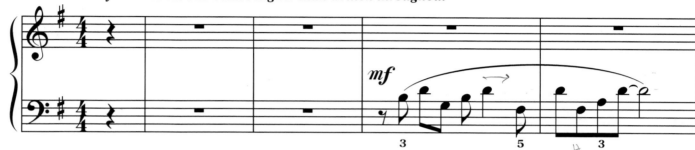

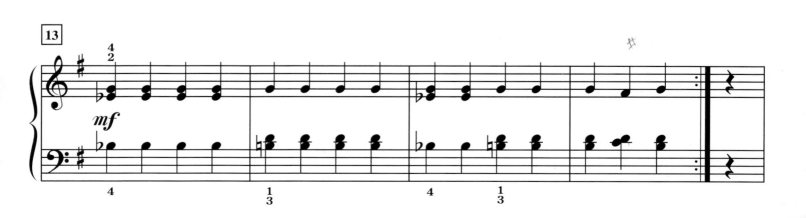

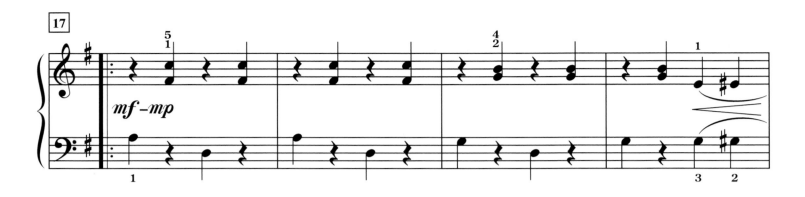

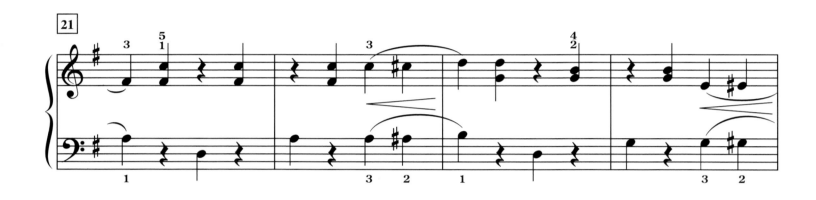

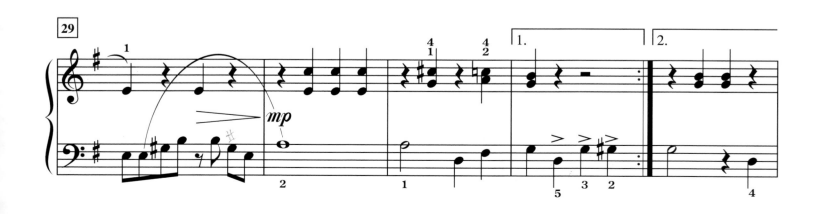

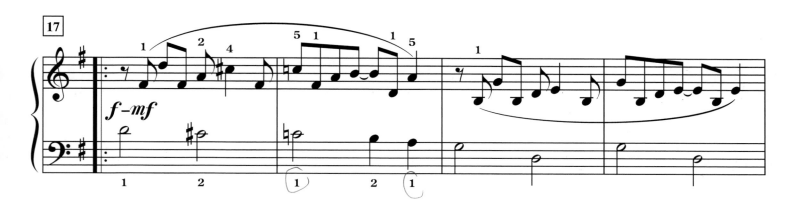

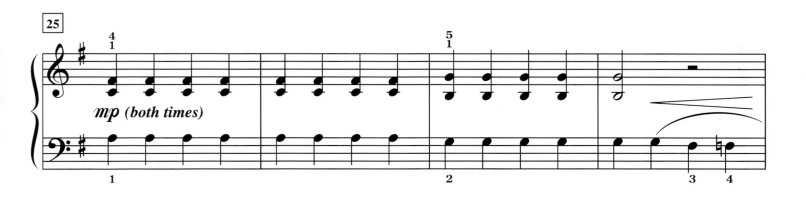

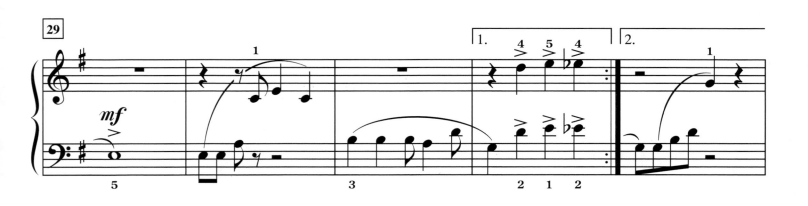

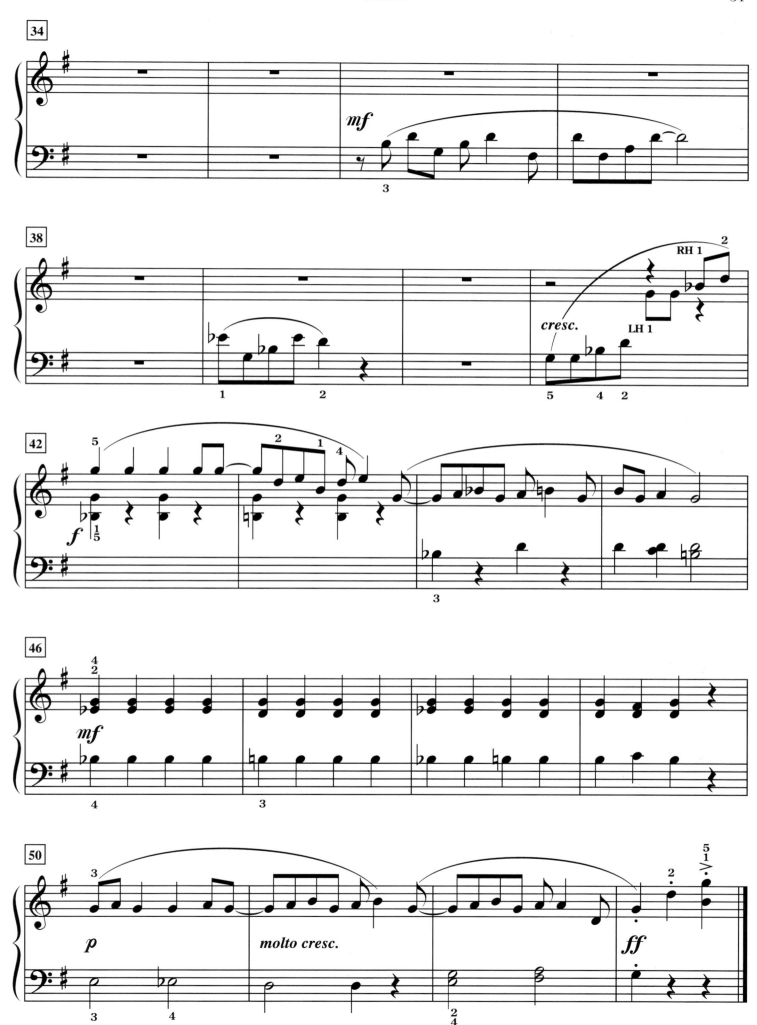